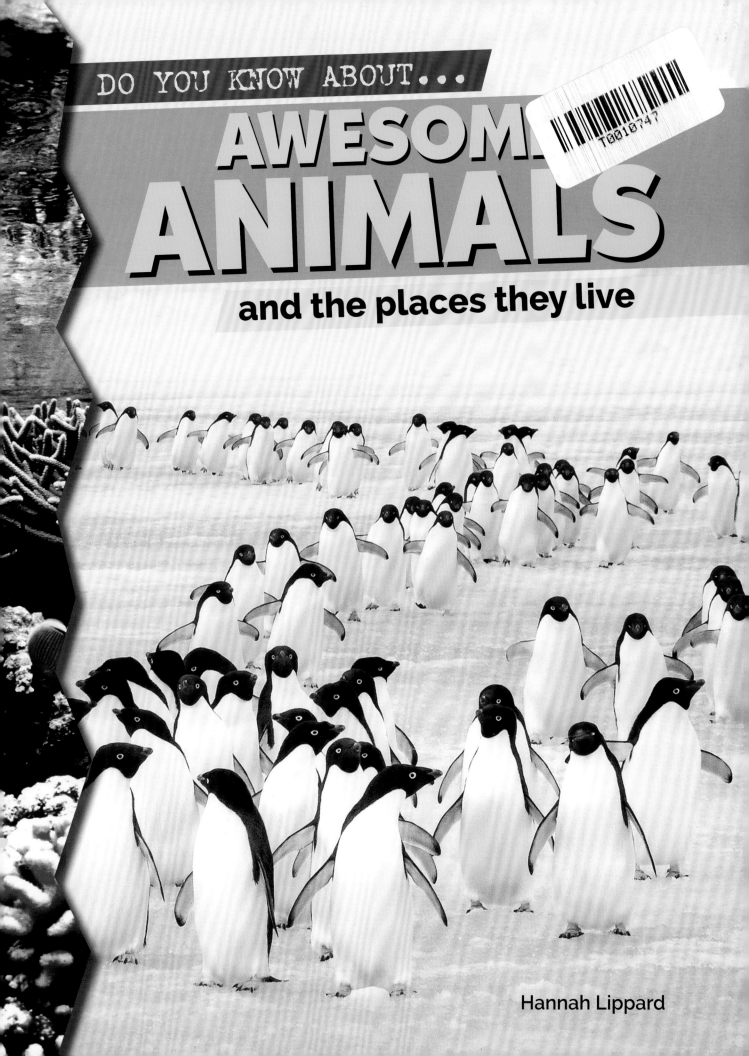

DO YOU KNOW ABOUT...

AWESOME ANIMALS

and the places they live

Hannah Lippard

Photo Credits

Key: (t) top; (tl) top left; (tr) top right; (m) middle; (ml) middle left; (mr) middle right; (b) bottom; (bl) bottom left; (br) bottom right

P6: World_map_with_equator (m); P7: Grib_skov (tr) File_by_Alexander_Baranov_-_ (5251916217) (m) Mosquito_2007-2 (bl); P8: Blue_Blue_Sea_-_panoramio (tr) Colpophyllia_natans_(Boulder_Brain_Coral)_entire_colony (ml) Coral_reef_at_palmyra.jpg (ml) Grimpoteuthis_bathynectes (mr) Octopus_vulgaris2 (br); P9: Green_Sea_Turtle_grazing_seagrass (tl) Sea_turtle_eggs_(7537674502) (tl) Whale_shark,_Rhincodon_typus,_at_Daedalus_in_the_Egyptian_Red_Sea._(35827412321) (mr) Aurelia_aurita_(Cnidaria)_Luc_Viatou (bl); P10: Expl1181_-_Flickr_-_NOAA_Photo_Library (tr) BMC_-_Diceratiidae-Diceratias.trilobus (mr) Architeuthis_dux_Verrill_1882 (bl); P11: Myctophum_affine (tr) Lanternfish_larva (tr) Eurypharynx_pelecanoides (ml) Riftia_tube_worm_colony_Galapagos_2011 (br); P12: Lago_Nahuel_Huapi (tr) Rainbow_Trout_(Oncorhynchus_mykiss) (mr) RainbowTrout (mr) Bachforelle_osmoregulatoin_bw_e (ml) Osmoseragulation_Carangoides_bartholomaei_bw_en (mr); P13: Red_freshwater_crab_DSC_1032 (tl) Geothelphusa_dehaani_ (9527479017) (tl) North_American_River_Otter_-_CNP_3336_(6910886576) (bl) North_American_River_Otter_(Lontra_canadensis)_ (6998574031) (br); P14: Mangrove_Cave (tr) Heron_tricol_01 (ml) Yellow_Bittern_hunting (mr); P15: Bobcat_(Lynx_rufus)_ (14045620728) (tr) Bobcat_(Lynx_rufus)_California (mr) Neurergus_microspilotus (ml) Taricha_torosa,_Napa_County,_CA (bl) Ragondin-myocastor-coypus (br); P16: Brazilian_amazon_rainforest (tr) Dendrobates-tinctorius-Epipedobates-tricolor (mr) Yellow-banded.poison.dart.frog.arp (ml) Ameerega_trivittata_(Madre_de_Dios,_Peru) (mr) Aras_Papagei (bl); P17: Jaguar_(Panthera_onca)_ male_drinking_..._(29175619965) (tl) Jaguar_(Panthera_onca_palustris)_male_Rio_Negro_2 (tr) The_Ghost_of_Darkness (mr) Two-toed_sloth_Costa_Rica (ml) Marius_Masalar_2016-09-19_(Unsplash) (br); P18: Autumnal_deciduous_forest_-_Laubwand_im_Herbst (tr) Great_spotted_woodpecker_(25780507403) (mr) Stock-photo-autumn-scenary-in-panorama-format-a-forest-in-vibrant-warm-colors-with-the-sun-shining-through-the-476548378 (ml) Cedrus_deodara_Manali_2 (mr) Fawn_3 (bl); P19: Porcupine_in_tree (tl) Tree_Climbing,_Bear_Style (ml); P20: Perovka_river,_Leningrad_oblast (tr) Gray_wolf_(Canis_Lupis) (mr) Howlsnow (ml) Snowshoe_Hare_(5728192736) (mr) Snowshoe_Hare-_Alert_(6990916044) (br); P21: 20070818-0001-strolling_reindeer (tl) The_Other_364_Days_of_the_Year-_The_Real_Lives_of_Wild_Reindeer_(15842503347) (tr) Canada_lynx_by_Michael_Zahra (ml); P22: Stipa_lessingiana_habitat (tr) American_Bison_AdF (ml) Elymus_cinereus_and_coyote_(5823378038) (bl) Coyote_at_Sonora_ Desert_Museum_Tucson_Arizona (br); P23: Greater_sage-grouse_(Centrocerus_urophasianus) (tr); P24: Three_Zebras_Drinking (ml) African_bush_elephant_ (mr) AElephantPlay2147 (bl); P25: White_rhinoceros_or_square-lipped_rhinoceros,_Ceratotherium_ simum_at_a_location_in_South_Africa_(15461073425) (tr) Queen_Elizabeth_Park,_Uganda_(15926687108) (ml) Fork-tailed_ Drongo,_Dicrurus_adsimilis,_at_Pilanesberg_National_Park,_South_Africa_(16047118271) (bl) Fork-tailed_Drongo_RWD (br); P26: The_Desert_Ultra_-_Low_Dunes (tr) Fennec_(Vulpes_zerda)_(5258215029) (mr) Suricates,_Namibia-2 (bl); P27: TiptonKangarooRat (tl)Camels_in_Wahiba_Sands_03 (mr) Chameau_de_bactriane (mr) Desert_iguana_(Dipsosaurus_dorsalis)_(20526299159) (br) P28: Antarctica_(8382309286) (tr) Penguin_in_Antarctica_jumping_out_of_the_water (mr) Polar_Bears_Across_the_Arctic_Face_Shorter_ Sea_Ice_Season_(29664357826)_(2) (bl); P29: Anim1754_-_Flickr_-_NOAA_Photo_Library (t) Pod_Monodon_monoceros (ml) Walrus_Cows_and_Yearlings_on_Ice (bl); P30: Everest_North_Face_toward_Base_Camp_Tibet_Luca_Galuzzi_2006 (tr) Vicugna-ESC (mr) Ailuropoda_melanoleuca_in_captivity_(4204834074) (bl); P31: Mountain_Gorilla,_Bwindi_(24490249134) (tr) Mountain_Goat_ Mount_Massive (ml) Female_Great_Horned_owl_on_her_nest (br); P32: Clouds_Zagreb_1 (tr) Bienen_im_Flug_52e_noise_removed (mr) Mexican_free-tailed_bats_exiting_Bracken_Bat_Cave_(8006832787) (mr) Tadarida_brasiliensis_2 (bl); P33: Bar-headed_goose_ Prasanna_Mamidala (tr) Southern_flying_squirrel (ml) Five-lined_Flying_Dragon_(Draco_quinquefasciatus)_(14163088876) (mr) Flying_lizard_(Draco_volans)_male (br); P34: Molehill-231386 (tr) Mr_Mole (mr) Groundhogs (mr) Marmota_monax_UL_04 (bl); P35: Earthworm_-_Flickr_-_treegrow (tr) Leptotyphlops_macrolepis (ml) Nine-banded_Armadillo (br); P36: Panthera_tigris_altaica_13_-_ Buffalo_Zoo (tr) Ngorongoro_Spitzmaulnashorn (ml) Orangutan_-_Sepilok_Sanctuary_Center_-_Sabah_-_Borneo_-_Malaysia_-_ panoramio_-_diego_cue (bl); P37: Astrochelys_radiata_-Roger_Williams_Park_Zoo,_USA-8a (tl) White_tiger_swim (mr) Red_Panda_ (25193861686) (bl); P38: Velociraptor_Wyoming_Dinosaur_Center (ml) Fred_Wierum_Velociraptor (ml) PSM_V01_D219_Mammoth (br); P39: Martha_last_passenger_pigeon_1914 (tr) Mershon's_The_Passenger_Pigeon_(frontispiece,_crop) (mr) Thylacinus (ml) Palaeopropithecus_ingens (br)P40: Baird's_Tapir_(Tapirus_bairdii)_(6788725593) (tr) Bald_Eagle_Fly_By_(30742412415) (ml) Green_ Chinese_dragon (mr) Licornedos (mr) 2012-natco-lion (br); P41: Saint-Aignan_(Loir-et-Cher)._Okapi (t) Koi_at_Japanese_Garden_-_ UH_Manoa_(5674161714) (m) Bairds-Tapir-Belize-Zoo-2010 (b); P42: Pygmy_Seahorse_-Lembeh_Straits (tr) Hippocampus_waleananu (ml) Chameleon_in_Nehru_Zoo_Park (mr) Calumma_parsonii,_Peyrieras_reptile_reserve_04 (bl); P43: Phasmatodea_00613 (tr) Peacock_flounder_Bothus_lunatus_(4672125450) (ml) Great_male_Leopard_in_South_Afrika-JD (mr) Giant_Leaf_Insect_(Phyllium_ giganteum)_(8758250810) (mr) Leopard_Tree_AdF (bl)

www.FlowerpotPress.com
CHC-0912-0476
ISBN: 978-1-4867-1653-1
Made in China/Fabriqué en Chine

Table of Contents

DO YOU KNOW ABOUT....

How much do you know about animals? Find awesome facts throughout the book as you learn more about the adaptive animals that survive and thrive in the wild. Just look for Do You Know About... facts throughout the book!

Earth's Diversity

There are about 7.7 million species of animals in the world! That means there are 7.7 million groups of animals that are so different from each other that scientists give them different names. Many of the differences between species have to do with the places they live.

Biodiversity

Biodiversity is the variety of living things. When a lot of different species live somewhere, that place is more biodiverse. Regions near Earth's equator are more biodiverse than regions near the poles. This is mostly because the equator is hotter than the poles. Biodiversity also changes with time.

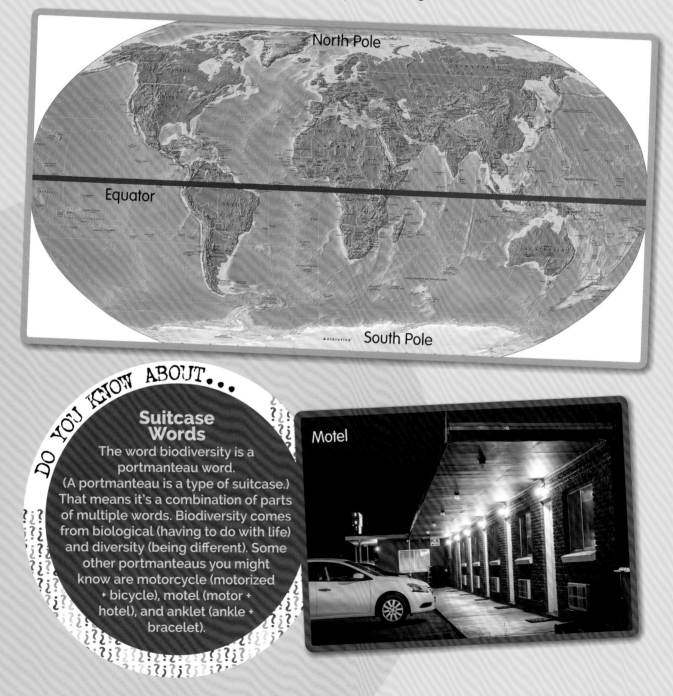

North Pole

Equator

South Pole

Antarctica

DO YOU KNOW ABOUT...

Suitcase Words

The word biodiversity is a portmanteau word. (A portmanteau is a type of suitcase.) That means it's a combination of parts of multiple words. Biodiversity comes from biological (having to do with life) and diversity (being different). Some other portmanteaus you might know are motorcycle (motorized + bicycle), motel (motor + hotel), and anklet (ankle + bracelet).

Motel

Habitats

A habitat is the place where an animal lives. Different animals need different types of habitats. An animal's habitat needs to have the right amount of shelter, water, food, and space. Some animals have needs that require them to live in a warmer climate, while other animals prefer a colder climate. Some of these animals have developed adaptations to help them survive in their habitat. However, if the habitat changes too much, the animal will no longer be able to live there.

DO YOU KNOW ABOUT...?

Parasites
A parasite is an animal whose habitat is another animal! This relationship hurts the second animal, called the host. The parasite lives on or in the host and uses it for food. Mosquitoes and fleas are considered parasites.

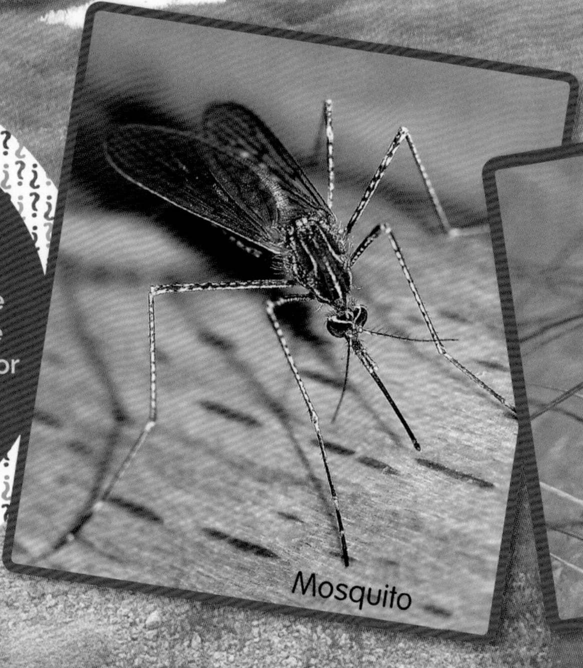

Mosquito

Flea

Ocean Animals

The ocean is one body of water that contains about 97 percent of Earth's water. It is usually divided into four parts: the Arctic Ocean, the Atlantic Ocean, the Indian Ocean, and the Pacific Ocean. Some animals, like fish, spend their whole lives in oceans. Others, like seabirds and sea turtles, live both on land and in the water.

Coral

An individual coral is a tiny animal called a polyp. Polyps have hard skeletons on the outside of their soft bodies. Most coral polyps live together in large colonies. Their skeletons build up over time and create coral reefs. Coral reefs are very important, because about 25 percent of ocean animals live in them. Corals eat by catching and killing zooplankton and small fish with their venomous tentacles.

Dumbo Octopus

Octopus

The body of an octopus is so soft that it can change shape. This lets the octopus fit into small spaces. When an octopus needs to move quickly, it propels itself with a jet of water. It can also release ink that makes the water dark and cloudy, so predators can't see it while it swims away. The octopus is believed to be the smartest invertebrate.

DO YOU KNOW ABOUT...

Reptiles vs. Fish

How can you tell if an animal is a reptile (like a sea turtle) or a fish (like a shark)? Reptiles have lungs, so they have to breathe air. Fish have gills, which let them take oxygen from the water. Also, reptiles have short legs, and fish have fins.

Common Octopus

Sea Turtle

Sea turtles hatch from eggs buried in the sand on beaches. Then they immediately crawl to the water. It is a very dangerous journey because animals like crabs and birds try to eat them on the way. Sea turtles are larger than freshwater turtles and tortoises, because living in the ocean means they have more room to grow and move. Sea turtles like to swim close to the surface or crawl onto the shore to warm themselves in the sunlight.

Shark

Most sharks are carnivorous, which means they eat other animals, and cold-blooded, which means their body temperature changes with the temperature of their environment. Sharks have multiple rows of teeth so that they can replace teeth they have lost! Their teeth are also specialized for their diet. Sharks can have narrow teeth for gripping, flat teeth for crushing, or sharp teeth for cutting. The whale shark is the largest fish in the world. It grows up to forty feet long.

DO YOU KNOW ABOUT...

Immortal Jellyfish

One species of jellyfish, the *Turritopsis dohrnii*, is biologically immortal. If it is hurt or sick, it can return to its polyp stage instead of dying. It does this by changing its cells into different types of cells. This process is called transdifferentiation.

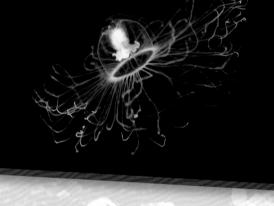

Immortal Jellyfish

Jellyfish

Jellyfish are made of about 95 percent water. They have two main body parts: the bell and the tentacles. The bell pulses to help them move. The tentacles sting other animals. Baby jellyfish develop into polyps, like coral. But polyps are only one stage of a jellyfish's life, and corals spend their whole lives as polyps. Adult jellyfish are called medusas. Scientists think jellyfish have existed for 600 or 700 million years—that's hundreds of millions of years before dinosaurs!

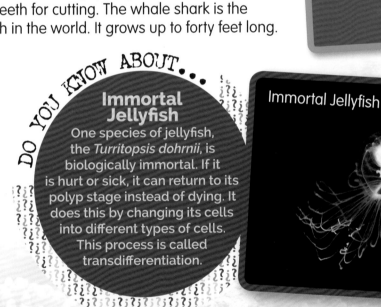

Deep Sea Animals

The deep sea is the deepest part of the ocean. It is so deep that it is almost or completely dark, because the sunlight cannot reach it. The animals living there need to be adapted to life with little light and high water pressure.

Deep-Sea Anglerfish

Deep-sea anglerfish can live a mile below the surface of the ocean. They have huge mouths full of sharp teeth that they can stretch to swallow animals twice their size! Part of an anglerfish's spine extends over its head and ends in a growth of flesh called a lure. Anglerfish move the lure to make it look like a small animal. The lure glows so it can attract prey in the dark.

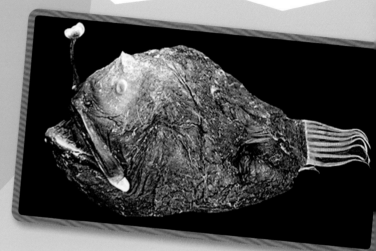

DO YOU KNOW ABOUT...

Glow-in-the-Dark Animals

When animals give off their own light, it is called bioluminescence. This light is usually blue or green. Sometimes bacteria living in the animal make the light and sometimes the animal makes the light itself. Many deep-sea animals are bioluminescent. Bioluminescence is rarer on land, but two examples are fireflies and glow worms.

Glow Worm

Giant Squid

Giant squids have enormous eyes, which are good for seeing in mostly-dark water. They have eight arms and two very long tentacles that help them hold their prey. Like octopuses, giant squid can propel themselves with a jet of water. The biggest giant squid ever found was fifty-nine feet long!

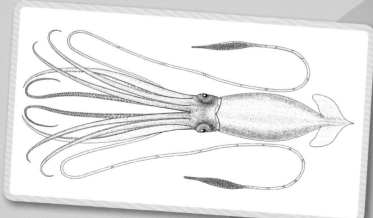

Lanternfish

Lanternfish are some of the most common fish in the ocean. They have special organs that create light. Different lanternfish species—there are at least 240—have different patterns of light. These patterns might help lanternfish communicate with each other. Some lanternfish move between deeper and shallower parts of the ocean. They spend the day in the dark, and then rise to higher levels at sundown.

Pelican Eel

The pelican eel is a black fish without any scales. It has such a big mouth that it can eat prey larger than itself. It also has a very long and thin tail that glows pink on the end. The end of the eel's tail is probably a lure for prey, like the lure of the anglerfish. Scientists think that pelican eels may find mates using their sense of smell and die soon after they reproduce.

DO YOU KNOW ABOUT...

Deep-Sea Gigantism

Animals in the deep sea tend to be larger than those that live in shallower parts of the ocean. This is called deep-sea gigantism. Scientists think it is caused by the colder temperatures or higher pressure in the deep sea.

Goliath Grouper

Giant Tube Worm

Baby giant tube worms can swim, but when they are adults, they no longer move. One end of the worm attaches to the ocean floor and the other end has a red organ called a plume. They live near hydrothermal vents that emit very hot water and minerals. Giant tube worms do not have mouths or stomachs, so they get food from bacteria that live inside them. This mutually beneficial relationship is called mutualism. Giant tube worms can be taller than adult humans!

Freshwater Animals

Fresh water is only about 2 percent of the water on Earth, but many animals depend on it to survive. Fresh water can be found in places like lakes, ponds, and rivers. It is called "fresh" because it has much less salt dissolved in it than ocean water.

Rainbow Trout

Rainbow trout are multicolored: usually green, pink, white, and black. Some rainbow trout spend their whole lives in fresh water, and others migrate between freshwater and saltwater ecosystems. Rainbow trout that migrate to the ocean are more silvery colored and called steelheads. They return to rivers to spawn.

DO YOU KNOW ABOUT...

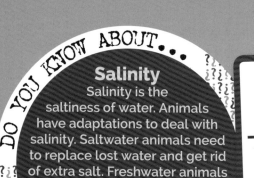

Salinity
Salinity is the saltiness of water. Animals have adaptations to deal with salinity. Saltwater animals need to replace lost water and get rid of extra salt. Freshwater animals need to replace lost salt and get rid of extra water. Animals do this through their kidneys, gills, or glands.

active ion absorbtion thru gilts

water intake thru skin

food

→ direction for transfer of ions (Na$^+$, K$^+$, Cl$^-$)
→ direction for transfer of ions

diluted urine

water loss over skin

drinks seawater

active ion depuration thru gilts

salty urine (Mg^{2+}, SO$_4^{2-}$)

River Dolphin

River dolphins live in South America and South Asia. They are smaller than ocean dolphins and have less blubber, because river water is shallow and warm. They also depend on hearing more than sight to catch prey, because the water is very muddy. River dolphins use their tail fins to swim forward and their flippers to steer.

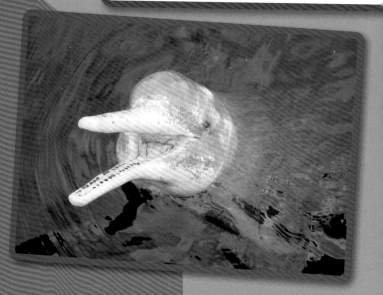

Red Freshwater Crab

Freshwater Crab

Freshwater Crab

Freshwater crabs live in tropical and subtropical regions. They can be found in rivers and streams, swamps, ponds, and even caves. Freshwater crabs have gills to breathe underwater. Sometimes their gills are modified to function like lungs so they can also breathe air! Freshwater crabs do not have as many offspring as ocean crabs. They also stay in a smaller area.

Alligator

Alligators are reptiles with thick scaly skin. There are only two living species of alligator: the American alligator and the Chinese alligator. Alligators have very strong muscles in their jaws for biting. They eat a variety of other animals, including fish, rodents, turtles, birds, and deer. Some alligators can grow over nineteen feet long and live more than fifty or even seventy years.

American Alligator

DO YOU KNOW ABOUT...

Alligators and Crocodiles

There are ways to tell alligators and crocodiles apart. Alligators are usually smaller, darker-colored, and faster than crocodiles. Alligators live in fresh water. Crocodiles live in salt water. Alligators have wide snouts. Crocodile snouts are pointy. Alligators live in the United States and China. Crocodiles live all over the world. Florida is the only place where alligators and crocodiles live together!

Crocodile

North American River Otter

North American river otters live in rivers, lakes, marshes, and more. Their long sensitive whiskers help them find food in the water. River otters have water-repellent fur, strong flat tails, webbed feet, and muscular bodies, making them excellent swimmers. They are very playful and they like to slide in mud and snow.

Wetland Animals

A wetland is like a cross between a water habitat and a land habitat. The soil in a wetland is so wet that aquatic animals and plants can live there. There are many names for different types of wetlands: marshes, estuaries, fens, swamps, bogs, and more.

Heron

Herons have long necks, long legs, and long beaks. They live on every continent except Antarctica, which is too cold for them. Herons do not swim, but their food does. They lurk on the edge of the water and stab prey like fish and crabs when it moves close enough. Some herons also use their big wings to either scare prey or attract it to the shade where they can catch it more easily.

DO YOU KNOW ABOUT...

Retractable Necks

Most birds with long necks fly with their necks outstretched. But herons have about twenty bones in their necks that are specially shaped. This lets a heron bend its neck like an S, until it is completely retracted.

Yellow Bittern

Platypus

Platypuses are so unusual-looking that scientists about 300 years ago thought they were fake. They look like a combination of different animals. They have bills and webbed feet like ducks, tails like beavers, and furry bodies like otters. Platypuses live in Australia. They are one of the only mammals to lay eggs. They also use electrical signals instead of smell or sight to find prey. And male platypuses have venom in their back feet!

Bobcat Adaptability
Bobcats are very adaptable to different environments. They live in swamps, deserts, forests, and even outside cities. There are more bobcats in the United States than any other type of wildcat. But people do not see bobcats very often, because they avoid humans and hunt at night.

Bobcat

Bobcats live in Canada, the United States, and Mexico. They have tufted ears, ruffs on the sides of their faces, and stubby tails. They are about twice the size of a house cat. Bobcats live alone except when raising kittens. Mother bobcats train their kittens to hunt for animals like rabbits and birds. After about a year, the kittens are ready to leave the den.

Spotted Salamander

California Newt

Newt

Newts are born in the water. Then they spend one to three years on land as juveniles and the rest of their lives back in the water. This means they are semiaquatic. Newts can regenerate their limbs, tails, and eyes. They can even regenerate some internal organs like their hearts and intestines. Some newts secrete toxins through their skin. One species of newt makes so many toxins that it can kill humans.

Coypu

Coypus, like newts, are semiaquatic. They live near fresh water or in wetlands, and they can stay underwater up to five minutes. Coypus are omnivores, which means they eat both plants and animals, but they like aquatic plants best. Coypus are a type of rodent, like mice and rats, but they are much larger. A big coypu can weigh over twenty pounds. Coypus have large, bright orange front teeth.

15

Rain Forest Animals

Rain forests are forests with high rainfall. They cover less than 2 percent of the planet, but they are extremely biodiverse. About half of all plants and animals are indigenous to rain forests.

Poison Dart Frog

Poison dart frogs live in tropical rain forests in Central America and South America. They are usually small, colorful, and toxic. Their bright colors warn animals that might want to eat them that they are poisonous. Scientists think the toxins in poison dart frogs' skin come from their food—bugs like ants and termites.

DO YOU KNOW ABOUT...

The Frog Life Cycle

Poison dart frogs hatch from tiny eggs covered in a protective jelly-like material. When they first hatch on the rain forest floor, they are tadpoles. Tadpoles have long tails and gills to breathe in the water like fish. Poison dart frog mothers carry their tadpoles on their backs to plants that collect rainwater. The tadpoles live in the pools of water while they grow. To become adult frogs, they have to develop lungs and legs. This process is called metamorphosis.

Macaw

Macaws are a type of parrot. They have colorful feathers, long tails, and strong beaks for opening nuts and seeds. They also lick clay from river banks. They might do this because the clay is high in salt content that helps balance their diet. Macaws are social birds that flock together and squawk loudly to communicate. Some macaws can imitate human speech.

Jaguar

The jaguar is the biggest cat in South America. It has yellow fur with black spots called rosettes because of their flower-like shape. Jaguars are carnivores. They can climb trees to attack terrestrial prey from above or swim in rivers to hunt aquatic prey like fish and turtles. Sometimes they swim across the Panama Canal, which can be over one hundred feet wide.

DO YOU KNOW ABOUT...

Black Panthers

The word "panther" can be another name for a cougar or mountain lion, but "black panther" refers to jaguars and leopards! Melanin is a black pigment that black panthers have more of than non-melanistic leopards. (Melanism is the opposite of albinism.) Black panthers still have spots, but they cannot be seen because of the extra melanin.

Sloth

Sloths, like poison dart frogs, live in Central and South American tropical rain forests. They spend most of their time hanging upside down in trees. They are herbivores, which means they eat plants. Sloths are very slow. They only travel six to eight feet in a minute to conserve energy, and they sleep up to twenty hours a day. Green algae often grows on their fur. It is a mutualistic relationship, because the algae camouflages the sloth and the sloth gives the algae a place to live.

Python

Pythons are some of the biggest snakes in the world, but they are nonvenomous. They hold onto their prey with their sharp teeth and then coil their body around it. This is called constriction. The prey animal dies because it cannot breathe and its heart cannot pump blood. Unlike some other snakes, pythons lay eggs.

Temperate forests are named for their location: temperate regions, the areas between the tropical and polar regions. Temperate forests have mild seasonal changes, a lot of rain, and fertile soil. There are temperate deciduous forests, temperate coniferous forests, and even temperate rain forests.

Woodpecker

Woodpeckers are birds known for the tapping sound they make with their beak. They drum quick patterns on hard surfaces to communicate with other woodpeckers. Woodpeckers mostly eat insects they find in trees. Because they can dig into the trunk to find bugs, some woodpeckers also eat tree sap. Many woodpeckers build their nests in tree trunks, too.

DO YOU KNOW ABOUT...

Coniferous Forests

The trees in deciduous forests lose their leaves every year. The leaves might change color to orange or red before they fall. The trees in coniferous forests do not lose their leaves. They are called evergreens because they stay green all year.

Deciduous Forest

Coniferous Forest

Deer

Deer are ungulates, or animals with hooves. Almost all male deer have antlers, and most female deer do not. Antlers are made out of bone and they are attached to a deer's skull. Every year deer shed their antlers and then regrow them. They use their antlers for fighting and attracting mates. Baby deer are called fawns. Most of them have white spots on their fur that help them stay hidden from predators.

Porcupine

Porcupines are rodents that have quills embedded in their skin. The quills are modified hairs with a hard covering and a pointed tip. They fall out when they come in contact with something else, and the porcupine grows new ones. Some porcupines in the Americas live in trees. They eat plants like leaves, bark, seeds, and berries.

Red Fox

Red foxes live most anywhere in the northern hemisphere. They are the largest species of fox, and their fluffy tails are more than half as long as their heads and bodies. Most red foxes have red fur, but there are color variations. Some red foxes have two dark stripes that make a cross shape, and they are called cross foxes. About 10 percent of red foxes are entirely silvery or black. They are called silver foxes. Red foxes have twenty-eight different calls to communicate with each other.

American Black Bear

American black bears can weigh up to 900 pounds. They are very good at climbing trees and they have a good sense of smell. Black bears mostly eat plants like grasses, berries, and nuts. Sometimes they also eat insects, fish, animals that are already dead, or even human food that has been thrown away. In the winter, American black bears hibernate in dens.

DO YOU KNOW ABOUT...

Hibernation

During hibernation, black bears sleep for months without food or water. This is possible because their heart rate and metabolic rate (how much energy they use) decrease. They dig dens in places like caves and hollow trees. Bears and other hibernating animals hibernate to save energy because there is less food available during the winter.

Taiga Animals

Taigas are located in the subarctic region: north of the temperate region but below the northern polar region. Taigas are also called boreal forests or snow forests. The trees in taigas are mostly coniferous, like pine and fir trees. Taigas have long and cold winters. It gets so cold that the soil can freeze.

Gray Wolf

Gray wolves are larger than all other wolves, dogs, and foxes. They can weigh as much as adult humans. They have thick and fluffy fur. Gray wolves in northern areas like taigas sometimes have white fur. They are very social and live in groups called packs that can include anywhere from two to thirty-six wolves. The leaders of the pack are called the alphas.

DO YOU KNOW ABOUT...

Howling

Gray wolves, like other wolves and dogs, can howl to communicate. Howling can be between members of the same pack to find each other or gather for hunting. It can also be between different packs to communicate about where their territories are.

Snowshoe Hare

The snowshoe hare has big furry back feet that keep it warm in cold weather and help it walk and hop on the snow. It thumps its feet against the ground to communicate with other hares. A snowshoe hare's fur changes colors, from brown in the summer to white in the winter. This helps it blend in with its surroundings during the different seasons.

Reindeer

Reindeer are a species of deer. In North America, they are usually called caribou. They are the only deer species where both male and female animals grow antlers. Reindeer can smell food, like lichens, buried under the snow, and their hooves are adapted for walking on snow. Some reindeer migrate in the spring and fall. They can travel thousands of miles in a year.

Canada Lynx

The Canada lynx lives in Canada and parts of the United States. It has fluffy gray and brown fur, with black tufts in its ears, a short tail with a black tip, and big furry paws for walking on snow. The Canada lynx's favorite food is the snowshoe hare, so the lynxes hunt at night when the hares are awake.

DO YOU KNOW ABOUT...

Migration

Migration is when a group of animals leaves one habitat and moves to a different one. Animals migrate because of the climate, food availability, or mating time. Many animals migrate seasonally, which means that they live in a warmer place during the winter and a cooler place during the summer.

Arctic Tern

Arctic terns are seabirds that eat small fish and crustaceans. They fly over the water and dive down to catch prey. They have white, gray, and black feathers and bright red beaks and feet. Arctic terns have the farthest migration of any animal. Every year they fly from their northern homes to Antarctica and then back again after six months. They can travel 40,000 or 50,000 miles in a year. That adds up to the distance of three trips to the Moon during their lifetime!

Grassland Animals

Grasslands are places where the main plants are grasses instead of trees. They have temperate climates, like temperate forests, and a medium amount of rain. Wetter grasslands have taller grass, and dryer grasslands have shorter grass.

American Bison

Bison are the largest land animals in North America. They can weigh over 2,000 pounds. Bison eat mostly grass and live in groups called herds. They have heavier fur in the winter, which they shed in the spring by rolling around on the ground. Bison especially like to roll around in dirt and mud. This can keep them cool and help soothe their skin if they have bug bites. All bison have horns.

DO YOU KNOW ABOUT...

Horns

Horns are different from antlers because they are permanent. Antlers are entirely made of bone and are shed every year. Horns are only bone on the inside, and they keep growing until the animal dies.

Antlers

Horns

Coyote

Coyotes are smaller than wolves and larger than foxes. They are social like wolves, but they do not live in packs. Coyotes will eat plants if necessary, but the majority of their diet is other mammals. They eat animals like rabbits, mice, birds, and occasionally deer. Sometimes coyotes partner with badgers for hunting. Coyotes can run quickly, jump high, and swim, but they cannot dig well like badgers can.

Greater Sage-Grouse

The greater sage-grouse is the largest grouse, a type of bird that lives on the ground. They must live in areas with sagebrush, a type of shrub. Sage-grouse use the sagebrush for both shelter and food. In the spring, male greater sage-grouse form groups called leks and strut around to impress the female sage-grouse. The males have sacs on their necks that expand to attract mates.

Prairie Dog

Prairie dogs are not dogs—they are rodents. They are named for a warning sound they make that sounds like a dog barking. They eat mostly grasses, roots, and seeds. Prairie dogs live in family groups in burrows underground. Their burrows have multiple chambers and entrances connected with tunnels. Sometimes prairie dogs dig networks of burrows called towns that are home to multiple prairie dog families and cover over 25,000 square miles.

DO YOU KNOW ABOUT...

Sexual Dimorphism

Sexual dimorphism occurs when animals of the same species but different sexes have different appearances. For example, only male sage-grouse have neck sacs, and only female red kangaroos have joey pouches. Often sexual dimorphism has to do with size—one sex might be larger than another.

Red Kangaroo

Red kangaroos live in Australia. They are the largest marsupial, a type of animal that carries its young in a pouch. Baby kangaroos are called joeys. They are very tiny when they are born and they live in their mother's pouch until they are big enough to walk around on their own. Adult male red kangaroos have reddish brown fur and females have gray fur. All red kangaroos have strong back legs and tails for jumping.

Savanna Animals

A savanna is like a mix between a forest and a grassland. The trees are more widely spaced than in a forest, so enough sunlight can shine on the ground for it to be covered with grasses. Savannas have dry and rainy seasons. During the dry season, there can be fires.

Zebra

Zebras are African animals related to horses that live together in herds. They eat grass together and groom each other, and if one zebra is attacked, other zebras will come help it. Every zebra has a different pattern of stripes. The stripes might be for camouflage, so that when zebras stand in a group they appear to blend together and predators cannot choose one to attack. Their stripes might also help the zebra avoid insects or stay cool.

DO YOU KNOW ABOUT...

Keystone Species

Elephants are a keystone species, which means they are very influential in their ecosystem. They can uproot entire trees and change a habitat. They also have a mutualistic relationship with some birds. The birds eat parasites that live on the elephant, giving the bird something to eat and relieving the elephant of the insects.

African Elephant

African elephants are the largest living land animal. They have long trunks that they use to breathe, carry water, and hold onto things. They also have tusks that they use for fighting and digging and big ear flaps that cool them down. Elephants eat plants like leaves and fruit.

White Rhinoceros

The white rhinoceros lives in Southern Africa. It has two horns on its nose, one short and one long. These horns are different from bison horns and deer antlers, because they do not contain any bone. White rhinoceroses eat grass. In the winter, they are active during the day. In the summer, they are crepuscular, or active around sunrise and sunset, to avoid the heat.

DO YOU KNOW ABOUT...

Keratin

Keratin is a type of protein. It is very strong. Rhinoceros horns are made entirely out of keratin. Bison horns have a keratin outer layer and a bone inner layer. Keratin can also be found in the hooves of ungulates as a hard covering over their toes. Cats' claws are made of keratin, too.

Giraffe

Giraffes are the tallest mammals in the world. Male giraffes are almost nineteen feet tall. They have long blue-black tongues—about eighteen inches long—that can hold onto food. Giraffes have ossicones on their heads, which look like horns but are covered in skin and fur. Their necks are so long that they can eat food other animals cannot reach, like the leaves at the tops of trees. Giraffes fight using their necks, which is called necking.

Fork-Tailed Drongo

The fork-tailed drongo is a small black bird named for the shape of its tail. It eats insects. Sometimes fork-tailed drongos steal food from other animals, a practice called kleptoparasitism. They follow other birds and some mammals, like meerkats, and then make fake alarm calls when the animal finds food. When the animal abandons their food, the drongo steals it.

25

Desert Animals

Deserts are regions with very little precipitation. The ground is often sandy or rocky. Both plants and animals need special adaptations to survive the desert's harsh temperatures and lack of water.

Fennec Fox

The fennec fox is the smallest species of fox. It digs holes in the sand to use as dens. Fennec foxes sleep in their dens during the day and come out to hunt at night. They have very large ears that help them stay cool in the desert and can even hear prey like rodents and insects moving underground. Fennec foxes have fluffy and light-colored fur, which keeps them cool during the day and warm at night. Fur also protects their feet from the hot sand.

DO YOU KNOW ABOUT...

Nocturnal Animals

Many desert animals are nocturnal, including the fennec fox. It is hottest and driest when the sun is out, so if animals are active during the day, or diurnal, they lose more water. If they are active at night, they can conserve water.

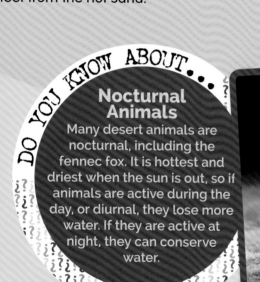

Meerkat

The meerkat is a mammal that lives in Africa. It has big claws for burrowing and for digging for insects and other small animals to eat. Meerkats are very social and they live in large colonies. When they are out of their burrows looking for food, one member of their group acts as a lookout for predators. Different meerkats in the foraging group take turns being the lookout.

Kangaroo Rat

Kangaroo rats hop on two feet, which is how they got their name. They can travel up to nine feet in one jump. Kangaroo rats live in burrows under the sand. Some species do not need to drink water at all, because they get it from the seeds they eat. This helps them survive in the dry desert.

Dromedary Camel

Camel

All camels have humps on their back. Dromedary camels have one hump, and Bactrian camels have two humps. Most camels are dromedaries. Camels can survive months without food and more than a week without water. They have clear membranes over their eyes to protect them from sand. Their feet expand when they step, which makes it easier to walk in the desert.

DO YOU KNOW ABOUT...

Built-In Storage
Scientists originally thought that camels' humps were for storing water. Now they know they are for storing fat. If camels cannot find food, they can get energy from the fat in their humps. This causes the hump to droop.

Bactrian Camel

Desert Iguana

Desert iguanas are lizards that live in the southwestern United States and northern Mexico. They make burrows in the sand underneath bushes, especially the creosote bush. They can handle very high temperatures without retreating to their burrows, up to 115 degrees Fahrenheit. Desert iguanas eat mostly plants, and they especially like the creosote bush's yellow flowers.

Polar Animals

There are two polar regions. The area around the North Pole is called the Arctic, and the area around the South Pole is called Antarctica. The poles receive less sunlight than other regions, so they are extremely cold. In the summer, there is light all day long. In the winter, there is almost constant darkness.

Emperor Penguin

Emperor penguins live in Antarctica. They have mostly white and black feathers, with yellow on their chests and ears. Penguins are birds, but they do not fly. Instead, their wings work as flippers for swimming. At breeding time, female emperor penguins lay one egg and then go to the ocean to find food. While they are gone, male penguins incubate the egg, or keep it warm. When baby penguins hatch, they are gray and fluffy instead of sleek like their parents.

DO YOU KNOW ABOUT...

Axial Tilt

An axis is the line something turns around. Earth has two different axes: the axis for rotation and the axis for orbiting the Sun. The difference between these axes is called axial tilt. It means that Earth is at an angle. Because of axial tilt, the North and South Pole take turns being pointed toward the Sun. When a pole is pointed toward the Sun, that pole's hemisphere has summer.

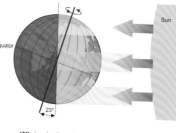

Summer in Northern hemisphere

Sun

Equator

23°

Winter in Southern hemisphere

Winter in Northern hemisphere

Sun

Equator

23°

Summer in Southern hemisphere

Polar Bear

Polar bears live in the Arctic. They are very large and covered in white fur. Their big furry feet help them walk on snow and ice and swim in the ocean. Polar bears eat mainly seals, which they hunt from ice on the sea. They are very good swimmers, but they need land and ice to survive. When the polar ice melts, their habitat shrinks.

Blue Whale

Blue whales are the largest animal to ever exist! They can be over one hundred feet long and weigh over 400,000 pounds. Blue whales live in oceans worldwide, including the Arctic Ocean and the water surrounding Antarctica. They eat mostly krill, a type of crustacean. In just one day, a blue whale can eat three or four tons of krill. Like all whales, blue whales have a blowhole on the top of their head that they breathe out of.

Narwhal

Narwhals are whales that live in the Arctic. Male narwhals have a single long, straight spiral tusk. Some female narwhals have tusks, too, and sometimes narwhals have two tusks. They might use their tusks to catch food, to fight, or to attract mates. Narwhals eat fish, squids, and crustaceans.

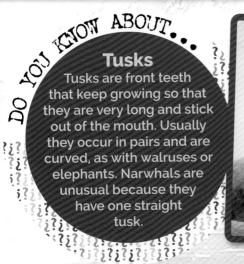

DO YOU KNOW ABOUT...

Tusks

Tusks are front teeth that keep growing so that they are very long and stick out of the mouth. Usually they occur in pairs and are curved, as with walruses or elephants. Narwhals are unusual because they have one straight tusk.

Walrus

Like narwhals, walruses live in the Arctic. They have two curved tusks that they can use to break and grip ice and to defend themselves. Their tusks are surrounded by whiskers that help them feel and identify objects. Walruses are very heavy because they have blubber under their skin to keep them warm.

Mountain Animals

Mountains are made from the movement of tectonic plates or from volcanoes. Usually they are part of mountain ranges. It is colder on the tops of mountains than at the bottom, so different kinds of animals live at different altitudes.

Vicuña

Vicuñas are wild animals related to llamas and alpacas. They are probably the ancestors of domesticated alpacas. They live in the Andes mountain range in South America. During the day they eat grass in the mountains' plains, and at night they sleep on the slopes. Vicuñas are small and can run very quickly and gracefully, even high in the mountains.

DO YOU KNOW ABOUT...
The World's Tallest Mountains
The thirty highest mountains in the world all come from two mountain ranges: the Himalayas and the Karakorams. They are all more than 25,000 feet tall. The Himalayas and the Karakorams are both located in central Asia.

The Himalayas

Giant Panda

Giant pandas are bears that live in mountain forests in China. Pandas have thick black-and-white fur. Their markings may camouflage them like the stripes of zebras. Giant pandas eat almost only bamboo for ten to twelve hours a day. In the winter, they move to lower and warmer elevations in the mountains instead of hibernating like black bears.

Mountain Gorilla

Mountain gorillas live in cold, misty forests on the dormant Virunga volcanoes in central Africa. Mountain gorillas have longer hair than other gorillas, which helps them survive cold mountain temperatures. They build nests out of plants in trees, on slopes, or on the ground. They groom each other when they are resting.

DO YOU KNOW ABOUT...

Altitude
Altitude is how high a place is. The weather changes at different altitudes, so different types of animals are better suited to living at different altitudes. Sometimes animals become isolated at a certain altitude because they cannot survive higher or lower.

Llamas

Mountain Goat

Mountain goats live in mountains in northwestern North America. Like giant pandas, they migrate to lower elevations during the winter. They have black horns with a ring around them for each year of their life, so counting the rings reveals the age of the goat. Mountain goats have large hooves and strong muscles for climbing steep rocky slopes without falling.

Great Horned Owl

Great horned owls live in the Americas, sometimes at elevations of over 10,000 feet. Great horned owls communicate by hooting. Most often, they hoot to find mates or to let other owls know where their territory is. Great horned owls live alone except when raising chicks. They frequently use nests built by other animals.

Animals in the Sky

The sky is everything above the earth's surface. Though technically the sky includes outer space, no animals can fly that high. They have to stay where there is enough oxygen, gravity, and air. Flying and gliding animals use their ability to travel and to escape danger.

Honey Bee

Honey bees live in colonies. A honey bee colony includes one queen bee, many female worker bees, and some male drone bees. The queen is the mother of most of the other bees. The workers have many jobs, including collecting nectar and pollen, while the drones mate with the queen. The colony lives together in a hive made out of beeswax. Honey bees make honey from the nectar they collect, which they store in the hive and use for food.

DO YOU KNOW ABOUT...

Echolocation
Echolocation helps Brazilian free-tailed bats navigate and find insects to eat. The bats emit sound waves and listen to the echoes, which show them where objects and prey are. Bats rely on echolocation much more than sight since they fly at night when it is dark.

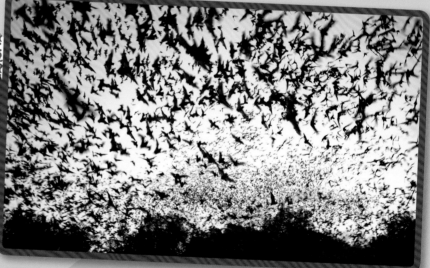

Brazilian Free-Tailed Bat

The Brazilian free-tailed bat lives in the Americas. They are called "free-tailed" because their long tails extend past the membrane connecting their feet. Their wings are pointed and narrow, which makes them fast fliers. They fly higher than any other bat, they can fly long-distance, and they even catch their prey while flying. Brazilian free-tailed bats usually roost in caves in huge groups. Like other small bats, Brazilian free-tailed bats use echolocation.

Bar-Headed Goose

The bar-headed goose lives in Asia. It is named after the black stripes on its head. It is one of the highest-flying birds in the world. Bar-headed geese regularly live at altitudes of 3,000 to 20,000 feet. When they migrate for the winter, they fly over the Himalayan mountains and have been reported at nearly 30,000 feet.

Flying Squirrel

Flying squirrels have membranes called patagia that stretch between their front and back legs. The patagia work like a parachute so that they can glide between trees, and they use their tails to brake. Flying squirrels can travel over 150 feet in one flight. Gliding allows them to escape quickly from predators and to forage for food more quickly than most squirrels.

DO YOU KNOW ABOUT...

Flying and Gliding

Bees, geese, and bats fly. Flying squirrels and flying lizards glide. What's the difference? Flying animals power their flight themselves by moving their wings. Gliding animals are technically falling. They use their membranes to slow the fall.

Flying Lizard

Flying lizards live in rain forests in South Asia. Like flying squirrels, they have patagia, but flying lizards' patagia are attached to their ribs instead of their wrists and ankles. Flying lizards glide by jumping from a tree and spreading their wing-like patagia. They usually glide about twenty-five feet after one jump. Although flying lizards spend most of their time in trees, they lay eggs in holes in the ground.

Animals Underground

Just like there are animals above the surface of Earth, there are animals below. They burrow or tunnel into the ground to make their homes, or they use the underground homes of other animals. These animals need special adaptations to live in places with low light and oxygen.

Mole

Moles have very small eyes and ears. They do not need well-developed eyesight, because it is dark in the burrows where they live. They have strong arms and paws with long claws to help them dig. Moles can breathe in air that has already been exhaled, so they can survive with less oxygen than other mammals.

DO YOU KNOW ABOUT....

Nicknames
Groundhogs go by many other names! The most popular is woodchuck. This comes from the Native American word *wuchak*, which means "the digger." Groundhogs are also called whistle pigs because of the sounds they make.

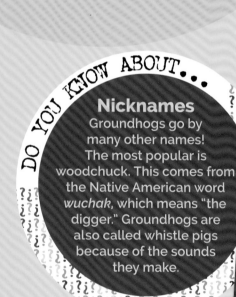

Groundhog

Groundhogs are rodents that sleep and hibernate in underground burrows. They usually have multiple burrow entrances, which makes it easier to escape predators. In the mornings and afternoons, they forage for food like clover and dandelions. If they are threatened, they can hide in their burrow or climb a tree. They make whistling sounds to warn other groundhogs of the danger.

Earthworm

Earthworms are invertebrates, so they have no skeleton. They are made up of segments covered in bristles that allow the worm to move. Earthworms can burrow down six-and-a-half feet in the ground. As they burrow, they eat dirt. The presence of earthworms makes soil more fertile and helps air move through it.

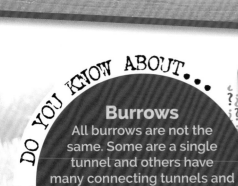

Blind Snake

Blind snakes are burrowing snakes with narrow bodies that are sometimes mistaken for earthworms if they are not very long. Their eyes are small and covered by scales on their head, so they cannot see very well. Blind snakes like to eat ants and termites. Sometimes they even live in the underground nests of ants and termites and eat their eggs.

DO YOU KNOW ABOUT...

Burrows

All burrows are not the same. Some are a single tunnel and others have many connecting tunnels and chambers. Animals may dig burrows in snow, dirt, sand, wood, and even rock. Some birds even make burrows instead of nests.

Armadillo

Armadillos live in the Americas, especially South America. They have armor made of bone on their back that protects them from predators, soil, and underground insects. Their stomachs are soft and hairy. Armadillos have large claws that they use to dig. The giant armadillo is the largest armadillo at 110 pounds, and the pink fairy armadillo is the smallest at three ounces.

Endangered Animals

Endangered animals are at a high risk of becoming extinct. Species become endangered when their population size or habitat is very small.

Black Rhinoceros

Black rhinoceroses live in a variety of habitats in Africa, including deserts, grasslands, and forests. They have smaller heads, ears, and horns than white rhinoceroses. They eat plants like leaves, branches, and grass, and their upper lip is pointed so it can hold the food while the rhino eats. Black rhinos are endangered because people kill them for their horns.

DO YOU KNOW ABOUT....

Competition
When two animals from different species need the same resources in a habitat, like food, they are in competition. African elephants are a competing species for black rhinoceroses because they eat the same plants the black rhinos do. Sometimes competition causes one species to decline, or sometimes one of the species adapts to use different resources.

Orangutan

Orangutans are apes that live in Malaysia and Indonesia. They have reddish-brown hair and long arms for swinging from trees. Every night, they build a new tree nest out of plants. The nests can be sixty feet above the ground. Orangutans rely on trees for shelter and for the fruit they eat. They are endangered because humans cut down the trees for wood and destroy their habitats.

Radiated Tortoise

The radiated tortoise lives in southern Madagascar. It has yellow star patterns on its shell. Unlike turtles, tortoises live on land. Radiated tortoises like to live in dry areas with brush or trees. They are endangered because people catch them to eat and to keep as pets. They are also losing their habitats.

Tiger

Most tigers have orange fur with black stripes. Some subspecies are white with brown or black stripes. Tigers like to eat hoofed animals like deer. They can leap over thirty feet to catch them. They are also very good at climbing and swimming. All tiger subspecies are endangered. They are hunted by humans and have lost most of their habitat.

DO YOU KNOW ABOUT...

Habitat Loss

Habitat loss occurs when a species can no longer live in a habitat. The animal will have to either find a new habitat or die. The main cause of habitat loss is humans using a habitat for farming. Another major cause is climate change. Habitat loss is the main reason for extinction around the world.

Red Panda

Red pandas live in forests in China and the Himalayan mountains. They eat bamboo like giant pandas, but they are not closely related to giant pandas. They have long bushy tails with rings on them that help them balance in trees. Red pandas are endangered because the forests they live in are being destroyed. This is called deforestation.

Extinct Animals

When all members of a species have died, the species becomes extinct. About 99.9 percent of all the species that have lived on Earth are now extinct. Species usually last less than ten million years.

Velociraptor

Velociraptors were dinosaurs that lived over eighty million years ago in the Cretaceous Period. Like all dinosaurs, they were reptiles. They were small, covered in feathers, and carnivorous. They had large claws on their back feet and many sharp teeth. Dinosaurs became extinct at the end of the Cretaceous Period during a mass extinction event. It may have been caused by an asteroid striking Earth and dramatically affecting the environment.

DO YOU KNOW ABOUT...

Mass Extinctions
In a mass extinction, many species become extinct around the same time. Biodiversity decreases quickly. There have been five mass extinctions. The sixth may be currently ongoing and caused by human activity.

Gastornis (Terror Bird)

Woolly Mammoth

The woolly mammoth lived at the same time as early humans. It was about the same size as an Asian elephant but covered in thick fur to protect it from the cold. Like elephants, woolly mammoths used their trunks and tusks as tools and weapons. Woolly mammoths may have gone extinct because they were hunted by humans.

Passenger Pigeon

Hundreds of years ago, there were billions of passenger pigeons in North America. They migrated constantly to look for food and shelter. Passenger pigeons flew in such huge flocks that their flight would block the sunlight. Starting in the 1800s, they were hunted by the thousands. Passenger pigeons became extinct in 1914.

DO YOU KNOW ABOUT...

De-Extinction

De-extinction means creating an animal from a species that is extinct. This could be done using the DNA remains of extinct animals, like passenger pigeons, to clone new animals. Some scientists think de-extinction is a bad idea because it is very expensive, and animals that are still alive need help.

Thylacine

The thylacine looked like a dog with stripes on its back. It was actually a marsupial, because it had a pouch like a kangaroo. Thylacines may have been able to balance on their back legs and tail like kangaroos, too. They became extinct during the 1900s, most likely because of hunting, habitat loss, and competition with dogs.

Sloth Lemur

Sloth lemurs lived on the island of Madagascar. Despite their name, they were not closely related to sloths. Sloth lemurs spent their time in trees, which they could hang from by their long arms and legs. They ate leaves, fruits, and seeds depending on the season and what food was available. Sloth lemurs may have become extinct about 500 years ago, probably because of hunting and changes to their habitat caused by humans.

National Animals

National animals are symbols that represent a country's culture, people, land, or history. Often national animals are native to the country, but sometimes the animal comes from somewhere else or is a mythical creature!

Bald Eagle

The bald eagle is the national bird of the United States of America. It has dark brown feathers, except for its head and tail, which are white. Bald eagles live throughout North America. They roost in tall trees near bodies of water because they eat fish such as rainbow trout, salmon, and catfish. Bald eagles spend most of their time resting, and when they fly, they beat their strong wings slowly so they can travel for a long time before they get tired.

DO YOU KNOW ABOUT...

Mythical National Animals

Some countries' national animals are mythical creatures. Here are some examples.
-Scotland: unicorn
-Bhutan: druk (thunder dragon)
-Indonesia: garuda (chimera)
-Greece: phoenix
-North Korea: chollima (flying horse)
-Wales: Welsh dragon
-China: Chinese dragon

Chinese Dragon

Unicorn

Lion

The lion is the most popular national animal. It is the national animal of at least fourteen different countries, including Belgium, Ethiopia, Iran, and Norway. Lions live in grasslands and savannas in Africa, along with one forest in India. Male lions have manes, which are extra hair that grows around their head and neck. Lions live in groups called prides that can include up to forty lions, but all the members are not usually together at once. To greet each other, lions rub their heads together.

Okapi

The okapi is the national animal of the Democratic Republic of the Congo, where they live exclusively in rain forests at medium altitudes. Okapis are most closely related to giraffes. Like giraffes, they have long black tongues that they use to browse for food like grass and tree leaves. Okapis mark trees in their territory by rubbing their necks against them. They also use their necks to show their social position.

Koi

The koi is the national fish of Japan. Koi are colorful versions of a fish called the Amur carp that lives in Asia. They are often calico-colored: red or orange, black, and white. When koi live in the wild, they eventually go back to their silver or gray coloring. Amur carps were originally believed to be a subspecies of the common carp, which comes from Europe, but they are a separate species native to Eastern Asia.

Baird's Tapir

The Baird's tapir is the national animal of Belize. It is similar in size to a donkey. Baird's tapirs live in Mexico, Central America, and parts of South America. They have proboscises, or long snouts, that they use to search for food. When foraging, they move in a zigzag pattern. Baird's tapirs are very good at running and swimming. They sleep in shallow holes with fresh water in them with their heads on their feet to keep them above the water. This helps them stay cool when it is hot and dry.

Animals in Disguise

Many animals have methods of disguising themselves to hide from other animals. This is called camouflage. Sometimes prey animals camouflage themselves to avoid predators. Sometimes predator animals camouflage themselves to sneak up on prey.

Seahorse

Seahorses are fish that live in shallow warm water around the world. They have tails that can grasp objects. Seahorses can change colors to match their environment. Some seahorses can even grow spots or protrusions to blend in with things like coral. Their camouflage abilities help protect them from predators like crabs, larger fish, and water birds.

DO YOU KNOW ABOUT...

Color Change

Animals that change color do so using tiny skin pigments called biochromes. Biochromes absorb and reflect different colors. Animals with a variety of different biochromes can change the color of their skin.

Chameleon

Chameleons live mostly in Africa. They can move their eyes separately from each other, and sometimes their tongues are longer than their bodies. They are best known for their color-changing abilities, which they use for communication more than disguise. Chameleons change color based on their moods and the conditions of their environment.

Stick and Leaf Insects

Stick and leaf insects camouflage themselves as sticks and leaves. They are usually green or brown. Leaf insects can even sway back and forth to look like a leaf swaying in the wind. These insects lay over one hundred eggs at once, and sometimes thousands. In addition to camouflage, some stick and leaf insects protect themselves using spines on their legs or toxic spray.

Stick Insect

Peacock Flounder

The peacock flounder is a flat fish that often lives in coral reefs. Both of its eyes are on the same side of its head. Peacock flounders can lie on the ocean floor and change colors to blend in with the sand. Then they wait for prey to swim by without noticing them. Their eyes are important for camouflage. If a peacock flounder cannot see, it cannot match itself to its environment.

DO YOU KNOW ABOUT...

Camouflage Techniques

Seahorses, peacock flounders, and stick and leaf insects use a technique called background matching—they make themselves look like their surroundings. Leopards use a technique called disruption. Their rosette patterns confuse animals looking at them and help them blend into the background.

Disruption

Leaf Insect

Background matching

Leopard

Leopards live in Asia and Africa. Like jaguars, they have yellow fur with dark rosettes. The rosettes help them sneak up on their prey unseen. Leopards are smaller than other big cats like jaguars, tigers, and lions. But they are so strong that they can carry the bodies of heavy prey like giraffes into trees.

Glossary

Adaptation – a change an animal makes to become better suited for its habitat

Albinism – the state of having very little dark pigmentation in the skin, feathers, or hair

Altitude – the height above sea level

Aquatic – living mainly or entirely in water

Biochrome – a color pigment in a plant or animal

Bioluminescence – light emitted by living organisms

Blubber – the fat of large ocean mammals

Camouflage – using disguise to stay hidden and unseen

Carnivore – an animal that eats animals

Climate – the weather conditions in a certain region

Colony – a group of animals of a species living together

Crepuscular – active during twilight

Crustacean – animals like lobsters and crabs that have exoskeletons and antennae

Deforestation – the destruction of forests

Diurnal – active in the day

Ecosystem – a community of organisms and the environment they live in

Equator – the circle around Earth that is halfway between the poles and divides the planet into two hemispheres

Extinct – not existing anymore

Forage – to search for food

Gravity – the force that pulls things toward the center of a planet

Hemisphere – a half of a planet as divided by the equator

Herbivore – an animal that eats plants

Hydrothermal vent – an opening in the earth's crust that emits hot water and minerals

Indigenous – native to a region and living there naturally

Invertebrate – an animal that does not have a spinal column or internal skeleton

Kleptoparasitism – when an animal takes prey or food caught by another animal

Lure – an object used to attract an animal so it can be caught

Mammal – a warm-blooded animal that feeds its young with milk and has hair on its skin

Marsupial – an animal that has a pouch for carrying its young

Melanism – the state of having more dark pigmentation than usual in the skin, feathers, or hair

Metamorphosis – a significant and rapid change in an animal's physical form

Migrate – to leave one habitat and then move to another

Mutualism – two animals of different species that are living together in a relationship that benefits them both

Nocturnal – active at night

Omnivore – an animal that eats both plants and animals

Orbit – to revolve around, as the planets do with the Sun

Parasite – an animal that lives in or on another animal in a relationship that benefits the first animal and hurts the second

Patagium – a membrane that helps an animal glide or fly

Pole – one of the ends of Earth's axis

Precipitation – water that comes from the sky in various forms, like rain, hail, and snow

Predator – an animal that preys on other animals for food

Prey – an animal that is caught by another animal and eaten

Proboscis – a long trunk or snout

Regenerate – to form or create again

Reptile – an animal that breathes air, has scales or plates, and moves on short legs or its stomach

Roost – to rest or sleep (refers especially to flying animals)

Semiaquatic – living in water sometimes or most of the time, and on land sometimes

Spawn – to lay eggs (refers specifically to aquatic animals)

Species – a group of animals that are genetically similar and can reproduce

Subspecies – a subgroup of a species that lives in a certain region and has some genetic differences from other members of the species but could still reproduce with them

Tectonic plates – enormous pieces of Earth's surface that move over time and whose movement can result in volcanoes, mountains, and earthquakes

Temperate – having to do with the temperate zone, a region between the tropics and the poles with a moderate climate

Terrestrial – living mainly or entirely on land

Toxin – a poisonous substance made by a living organism

Tropical – having to do with the tropics, a region around the equator

Ungulate – a hoofed mammal

Water pressure – the force of water against another object

Index